# The Mindfulness Beginner's Bible

*How to Live in the Present Moment, Relieve Stress and Find Happiness*

# Table of Contents

# Introduction

In recent years, mindfulness has become a buzzword in mainstream media, with regular features in magazines like *Fortune, Forbes, The New York Times,* and *The Huffington Post,* just to name a few. Today, mindfulness meditation is by far the most popular and most researched form of meditation in the West, and a growing number of people are embracing it every single day.

In this book you will learn exactly why mindfulness has become so popular over the years and why many highly successful people like Emma Watson, Angelina Jolie and Oprah Winfrey all incorporate the life-changing practice of mindfulness into their lives.

Mindfulness can seem a bit daunting at first, especially if you're not sure where to begin. However, the moment you recognize that mindfulness is not about trying to empty your mind, but rather about resting your awareness on your present experience, without effort, struggle or resistance, you begin to awaken and mindfulness becomes the most blissful, life-giving moment of the day.

*The Mindfulness Beginner's Bible* will teach you how to harness the power of the present moment by integrating mindfulness into your daily life. You will discover how mindfulness can have profound effects not just on your mind, but on virtually every aspect of your life – your body, relationships, health and even your career.

This book will take you by the hand and show you how step-by-step how to instill simple mindfulness techniques into your daily routine, inevitably leading you to a more successful, happier and healthier life. It will teach you a new way of engaging with the present moment, where you can access a higher level of consciousness that is beyond the mind.

# Chapter 1 - What is mindfulness?

## *"Life is a dance. Mindfulness is witnessing that dance."*
Amit Ray

Have you ever started eating a packet of chips and then suddenly realize that there is nothing left? This is one example of mindlessness that most of us experience on a daily basis. We, as humans often get so absorbed in our thoughts that we fail to experience what is happening right in front of us.

In modern society, most of us suffer from a condition called compulsive thinking. We have this hysterical inner voice that is constantly jumping from one thought to the next, obsessing about every little detail that could go wrong, complaining, comparing and criticizing everything and everyone. Sadly, most of us have become hostages to the whims of our minds, to the point where we even identify with the mind, thinking that we are our thoughts, when in reality we are the awareness behind our thoughts.

The moment you start observing your thoughts without identifying with them, you enter a higher level of consciousness beyond the mind and you reconnect with your true Self – the eternal part of you that is beyond the transient, ever- wavering physical realm.

Take a few seconds right now and become mindful of your hands. Feel the warmth that emanates from them. Rest your attention on every sensation in your hands. Feel your blood pulsing through them. Become one with your hands and notice the subtle tingling sensation as you become aware of them.

If you did this little exercise, I bet you noticed your mind becoming a bit more still. When you rest your attention on your body, you are living actively in the now. Awareness of the body instantly grounds you in the present moment and helps you awaken to a vast realm of consciousness beyond the mind, where all the things that truly matter - love, beauty, peace, creativity and joy - arise from.

Research has shown that we spend up to 50% of the time inside our heads - a state of mindlessness where we are continuously consumed by the chaotic impulses of our minds that are constantly thinking, ruminating the past and worrying about the future. Sadly, most people go through life in a walking haze, never really experiencing the present moment, which is our most precious asset.

Mindfulness is about being fully immersed into your inner and outer experience of the present moment. One of the best definitions of mindfulness is provided by the mindfulness teacher Jon Kabat-Zinn: *"Mindfulness means paying attention in a particular way; On purpose, in the present moment, and non-judgmentally."*

Jon Kabat-Zinn breaks down mindfulness into its fundamental components: In mindfulness, our attention is held...

## *On purpose*

Paying attention on purpose means intentionally directing your awareness. It goes beyond merely being aware of something. It means deliberately focusing your conscious awareness wherever you choose to, instead of being carried away in the perpetual storm of your thoughts.

Secondly, our attention is plunged...

### *In the Present Moment*

The mind's natural tendency is to wander away from the present and get lost in the past or the future.

Mindfulness requires being in complete non- resistance to the present moment.

Finally, our attention is held...

## *Non judgmentally*

In mindfulness there is no judgment, there is no labeling, there is no resistance and there is no attachment. You simply observe your thoughts, feelings and sensations as they arise without ever energizing with them. As soon as you realize that you are not your thoughts, but the observer behind your thoughts, they will immediately lose power over your.

Mindfulness goes beyond basic awareness of your present experience. You could be aware that you are drinking tea, for example, however mindfully drinking tea looks very different. When you are mindfully drinking tea, you are purposefully aware of the entire process of drinking tea – you feel the warmth of the cup, the subtleties in smell and taste of the tea, the sensation of heat as you press your lips against the cup... – you intentionally immerse yourself in every single sensory detail that makes up the experience of drinking tea, to the point where you completely dissolve into the activity.

Mindfulness is about maintaining the intention of being completely plunged into your experience, whether it is drinking tea, breathing or doing the dishes. You can bring mindfulness to virtually any activity in your life.

# Chapter 2 - The Power of the Present Moment

*"I have realized that the past and future are real illusions, that they exist in the present, which is what there is and all there is."* Alan Watts

When you think about it, the present moment is the only moment that really exists. The past and the future are merely persistent illusions – the past is obviously over, and the future hasn't happened yet. As the saying goes, *"Tomorrow never comes"*. The future is merely a mental construct that is always around the corner.

Even when you dwell on the past or worry about the future, you're doing so in the present moment. At the end of the day, the present moment is all you and I have, and to spend most of our time outside the present means we are never truly living. Spiritual leader Eckhart Tolle puts it beautifully: *"People don't realize that now is all there ever is; there is no past or future except as memory or anticipation in your mind."*

However, most people spend most of their waking time imprisoned within the walls of their own thoughts, usually in regret of the past or in fear of the future, which are two ways of not living at all.

The present is the only moment in our lives where we have complete control over our destiny. We can decide our course of action only in the now – we can make a new friend, start a new business, get back to the gym, decide to stop smoking... The present is the only moment where your creative power can be exercised; it is the only place where you have full control over your life. Embracing the present moment is the only way to live a happier, healthier and more fulfilling life. As Buddha said, *"The secret of health for both mind and body is not to mourn for the past, worry about the future, or anticipate troubles, but to live in the present moment wisely and earnestly."*

The biggest obstacle that keeps us from living in the present moment is the mind. Embracing mindfulness is a journey that requires practice and dedication, but it is a process that will inevitably lead you to a much happier and more fulfilling life where every moment is lived to the fullest. Here are 8 steps to start living in the present moment:

## Practice non-resistance

The first step towards living in the present is learning to live in acceptance. You must learn to accept your life as it is today, rather than wish it was any other way. You must come into complete non-resistance with your current experience of life. By letting go of the hold the past has over you, you free your mind from unproductive thoughts and you reclaim the present moment. As Eckhart Tolle says, *"Accept - then act. Whatever the present moment contains, accept it as if you had chosen it. Always work with it, not against it."*

## Focus on the Now

In order to live in the present moment, you must focus on what you are doing in the now, whatever it may be. If you are doing the dishes, then do the dishes. If you're eating dinner, then eat dinner. Don't view the seemingly mundane activities in your life as nuisances that you hurry to get out of the way. These moments are what our lives are made up of, and not being present in them means we are not truly living.

## Don't take your thoughts too seriously

Identification with the mind is the root of much unhappiness, disease and misery in the world. Most people have become so identified with their mental chatter that they become slaves to their own compulsive thoughts. Being unable to stop thinking and means we are never living in the present moment. When you learn to observe your thoughts as they come and go without identification, you step away from the chaotic impulses of the mind and you ground yourself in the now.

## Meditate

You don't have to meditate to be mindful, but research has shown that engaging in a regular meditation practice has a spillover effect on the rest of your life. When you meditate you essentially carry the state of stillness and awareness that you experience during your meditation session into the rest of your day. Meditation is practice for the rest of your life.

## Pay attention to the little things

Notice the seemingly insignificant things around you. Pay attention to nature for example. Notice the greenery around you - be grateful for every tree, every plant, every flower and realize that you could not survive without their presence. Go through your life as if everything is a miracle. From the majestic rising of the sun, to the chirping of birds outside your window, to the fact that your heart is beating every single second – life is truly a miracle to behold when you immerse yourself in the present moment.

## Do one thing at a time

Multitasking is the opposite of living in the now. When your attention is divided between several tasks like eating, driving, making a phone call, you cannot fully experience the present moment. Studies have shown that people who multitask take about 50% longer to complete a task with a 50% larger error rate. To be more mindful, you must become a single-tasker. When you're eating, just eat. When you're talking to people, just talk to them. Develop the habit of being completely immersed into whatever you're doing. Not only will you be more efficient, but you'll also be more alive.

## Don' try to quiet your mind

Living in the present moment does not require any special effort. The present moment is already at your fingertips. There is no need to expand energy to empty your mind. In mindfulness there is no stress, no struggle and no effort because you are not trying to force anything – you are in complete non- resistance to your current experience of life.

## Stop worrying about the future

Worry takes you out of the present moment and in the future into an infinite world of possibilities. You cannot worry about the future and simultaneously live in the present moment. Instead of worrying about things that may or may not happen, spend you time preparing to the best of your ability and let go of the rest. Worrying won't change the future, but it will definitely elevate the cortisol levels in your body and drain you of your vital energy.

# Chapter 3 -The Benefits of Mindfulness

*"The present moment, if you think about it, is the only time there is. No matter what time it is, it is always now."*
*Marianne Williamson*

Over the past decade, a vast amount of scientific research has been carried out to investigate the benefits of mindfulness for the human mind and body. Thousands of peer-reviewed studies have shown that practicing mindfulness has a wide range of benefits for the mind and body. Here are 24 noteworthy benefits of mindfulness:

- Improves well-being
- Reduces stress and anxiety
- Lowers blood pressure
- Boosts working memory
- Improves focus
- Increases mental and physical energy
- Lessens emotional reactivity
- Improves relationships with other people
- Increases empathy and compassion
- Reduces insomnia
- Increases understanding of one's self
- Develops a sense of self-acceptance and self-compassion
- Boosts cognitive function
- Sharpens memory, focus and attention
- Improves emotional intelligence
- Helps treat addictions
- Relieves stress
- Helps with weight loss
- Helps treat heart disease
- Improves sleep
- Deepens connection with all beings
- Reduces pain more effectively than morphine
- Treats long-term depression more effectively than drugs or counseling
- Helps treat eating disorders

Mindfulness involves paying attention to your current experience of life, whether it be a sound, a sight, a taste, a sensation, a thought or an emotion. It is a way to bring joy, happiness and wisdom into every moment of our lives. There are many reasons to incorporate mindfulness into your life, but here are 3 important ones:

# Let go of judgment

A key component of mindfulness is non-judgmental awareness of the present moment. In mindfulness you train yourself to be an impartial observer of whatever is happening in the now, without ever judging, labeling or evaluating anything. This attitude will transfer into your daily life and you will find yourself able to develop deeper and more meaningful relationships.

# Make better decisions

When we are carried away by the impulses of the mind, it's almost impossible to make level-headed decisions. In this state we are more emotionally reactive and tend to make decisions from a place of fear, which almost always end up being terrible decisions. Mindfulness allows us to become reflective instead of reactive – when we are mindful we are able to take a step back and choose the best course of action instead of emotionally responding to people and situations in a way that we regret later on.

# Be less egocentric

Most people spend their entire lives only thinking about themselves. Their mental dialogue is almost entirely self-focused: "When will I get what I want?" "What's in it for me?" "Why me?"... When you practice mindfulness, you step away from the whims of your egoic mind and you expand your awareness to the world around you. Practicing mindfulness increases the activity in neural networks in your brain involved in understanding the suffering of others, and thus fosters compassion and altruism. Mindfulness also trains you to be non-judgmental and non-reactive, which builds empathy.

# Chapter 4 - Mindfulness in Everyday Life

*"Drink your tea slowly and reverently, as if it is the axis on which the world earth revolves – slowly, evenly, without rushing toward the future. Live the actual moment. Only this moment is life."*
Thich Nhat Hanh

Mindfulness isn't something that you practice once and then forget about it. Mindfulness is a way of life and it can be incorporated into everything you do, as long as you are completely immersed in the present moment. Here are 5 ways to incorporate mindfulness into your everyday life:

## Embrace mundane tasks with mindfulness

Mindfulness be incorporated throughout your day just by paying more attention to whatever you are doing in the now. Instead of switching on auto- pilot when you do the dishes, laundry or clean the house, let the light of awareness shine on your seemingly boring activities and notice how they transform into therapeutic moments of your day.

## Take walks

Walking, especially through nature, is one of the best ways to quiet your mind, tap into your creativity and savor the miracle of the present moment. As spiritual leader Thich Nhat Hanh says, *"Walk as if you are kissing the Earth with your feet."* Walking is also an aerobic exercise that is proven to lead to a better mood, improved focus and creativity. Some studies have shown that a brief walk is as effective as antidepressants for mildly depressed patients as it makes the body release feel-good chemicals called endorphins, while at the same time reducing stress and anxiety.

## Know when to check your phone

In modern society, most of us have become addicted to constantly checking our phones for the latest update, text message, and Facebook comment. Scientists have shown that every time we check our phones our brains release dopamine, a neurochemical that causes us to continuously seek novel information. People who are mindful know when to check their phones and they understand how important it is to put away their mobile devices at times, especially when interacting and connecting with other people.

## Bring presence into your relationships

In today's fast moving world we rarely allow ourselves to spend time with the people we most care about. After a long day at work most of us go home to our families, and while we are physically there, our minds are elsewhere and we fail to really connect people around us. Being present in your relationships is not just about showing up physically, but it is about showing up mentally and emotionally as well. A brief moment spent in complete presence with your loved ones is worth more than a few hours spent thinking about the past or future. As Oprah Winfrey says, *"One of the greatest gifts you can give is your undivided attention."*

## Mindfully listen to others

Very few people have the ability to truly listen. Most of us "listen" by simply hearing the words, judging what is said and immediately thinking of what to say next. True listening goes far beyond just perceiving sound - it is about being completely present with the other person and listening to what they are saying as if it was the most important thing in the world. By mindfully listening to others, you bring stillness into your relationships and you connect with people on a much deeper level. Therapists are able to make a living out of listening to people; they are so skillful at listening that they enable their patients to liberate themselves from their worries, fears, and shackles of the past.

# Chapter 5 - 6 Common Mindfulness Myths

*"Realize deeply that the present moment is all you have. Make the NOW the primary focus of your life."*
Eckhart Tolle

Although mindfulness has become very popular in the western world, there still exist widespread misconceptions that prevent people from either getting started with mindfulness or developing it into a long-term practice. Here are 6 common mindfulness myths dismantled:

## Myth #1: Mindfulness is for religious or spiritual people

**Truth:** While mindfulness has been practiced within

various religious and spiritual traditions throughout history, mindfulness itself its not a religious activity. There is no religion, belief system or spiritual dogma associated with mindfulness. It is simply a practice for elevating your life by being fully engaged in the present moment. Mindfulness does not conflict with any religious or spiritual view and thus can be practiced by anybody.

## Myth #2: Mindfulness is escaping reality

**Truth:** Mindfulness is actually about facing reality. It helps you get a deeper understanding of your mind, how your thoughts influence your perceptions and how the impulses of your mind cause you and others suffering. Mindfulness is not an escape from reality but a voyage into the depths of your being where you gain higher levels of self-awareness and self-understanding, allowing you to bring clarity and wisdom into your life.

## Myth #3: Mindfulness is practiced only during meditation

**Truth:** There are several ways to incorporate mindfulness into your life. Many people like to carve out time to sit and have a formal mindfulness meditation session where they usually focus on their breathing. However, mindfulness can also be incorporated into the activities that you're already doing every single day – taking a shower, going to work, doing the dishes, eating dinner... The key is to find the right balance between a formal practice of mindfulness where you sit down and meditate and the informal practices where you simply become aware of what you are doing in the moment.

## Myth #4: It takes years to experience the benefits of mindfulness

**Truth:** You will start noticing big changes from practicing mindfulness sooner than you think. In 2011, Sara Lazar at Harvard University found that 8 weeks of mindfulness meditation significantly increased the size of the hippocampus, an area of the brain that governs learning and memory. She also found that mindfulness increased the size of certain areas of the brain involved in emotion regulation, and decreased the brain cell volume in the amygdala, which is responsible for emotions of fear, anxiety and stress.

## Myth #5: Mindfulness is about feeling good

**Truth:** While mindfulness will often make you feel the bliss of being grounded in the present moment, it will also take you to dark corners of your mind. You will become aware of thoughts and emotions inside of you that may be to difficult experience. It is not uncommon for people to cry during mindfulness meditation for example. This is a positive sign however, because being present provides the space for you to release unresolved negative emotions inside you, allowing you to make peace with the past and move forward with serenity.

## Myth #6: Meditation takes too much time

**Truth:** The reality is, the more you practice mindfulness, the more time you have: mindfulness revitalizes your body and mind, which allows you to go through the day more focused, more productive and less distracted. With mindfulness you are more efficient and thus you are able to accomplish more in less time The key is to realize how important mindfulness is to your life and to make it a priority.

# Chapter 6 - 5 Common Obstacles to Mindfulness

**"Keep knocking, and the joy inside will eventually open a window**
*and look out to see who's there."*
Rumi

Despite the incredible benefits that mindfulness has to offer, many people still fail to incorporate it into their daily lives. To make sure you do not become one of them, here are the 5 common obstacles to meditation and how you can overcome them:

## Obstacle #1: Outcome Orientation

One of the fundamental components of mindfulness is non-judgmental awareness. Mindfulness is a process where you must detach yourself from any kind of result. Your mindfulness practice should never be judged or evaluated in any way – judgment only creates more stress and more mental chatter. Be process oriented and profound benefits will inevitably come.

## Obstacle #2: Distractions

There are distractions everywhere in today's world. From the constant flow of advertisements to the pinging of email and text notifications on our phones - it can be tough to practice mindfulness when we have a million different things competing for our attention. The key is to discipline yourself to only focus on one thing at time – resisting distractions is a habit that you will only develop through practice.

## Obstacle #3: Perfectionism

Realize that there is no such thing as a perfect mindfulness practice. You will always have intrusive thoughts and moments of mindlessness when you try to practice mindfulness. Some days your mind will be quieter than others. That's totally normal. Do your best to stay in the present moment, but don't become obsessed with being perfectly mindful all the time.

## Obstacle #4:Discouragement

Anything worth doing takes practice and dedication. Mindfulness is no different. The key to developing a lifelong mindfulness practice is to realize the profound benefits it has to offer and use that as fuel to keep going when the going gets tough.

## Obstacle #5: Impatience

Understand that mindfulness is a life-long practice. Don't expect to become enlightened after two weeks of practicing mindfulness. Just like everything worth pursuing in life, it can take a bit of time to experience the full range of benefits that mindfulness has to offer.

# Chapter 7 - Mindfulness Techniques

*"Looking at beauty in the world is the first step of purifying the mind."*
*Amit Ray*

## Mindful Breathing

Mindful breathing is a simple but powerful technique where you intentionally rest your attention on your breath.

To practice mindful breathing, sit comfortably on a chair with an upright and relaxed posture. Then, purposefully direct your attention to the changing sensations of your breath. Become aware of the air flowing in and out of your nostrils. Notice how each breath is slightly different. Be aware of the subtle gap between your incoming and outcoming breath.

When thoughts pop up in your mind, observe them

without identifying with them; accept them as they are and gently return your attention to your breathing. Repeat this for the entire length of your meditation. You can start with as little as 5 minutes every day.

When your mindfulness session comes to an end, remain seated for a few minutes, breathe deeply into your diaphragm and let yourself receive your meditative experience before you gradually return to your daily activities.

## Mindful Listening

Meditation doesn't necessarily have to be practiced in complete silence. In fact, one of the most direct ways to connect with the present moment is to pay attention to the sounds around us. Even when there is noise, you can become aware of the stillness underneath the sounds. When you pay attention to the silence between the sounds, you create inner silence and you bring stillness into your mind.

You can practice mindful listening at any point throughout your day. Simply pay close attention to all the sounds that are reaching your ears. From the chirping of birds outside, to the rumbling sound of a truck passing by, to the passionate voices of people arguing next to you – immersing yourself in the depths of the sounds around you without ever judging them will instantly ground you in the present moment.

## Mindful Eating

Mindful eating involves taking in food with purpose and attention. To practice mindful eating, you must let the light of your awareness shine on the entire process of eating. Appreciate the appearance of your food, notice the subtle flavors, texture, smell and even the sound of the food inside your mouth. Chew your food slowly and reverently and be appreciative of the fact that you are able to stay alive by ingesting food. Practicing mindful eating has also been shown to reduce overeating, increase your enjoyment of food, improve your digestion and make you feel more satiated with less.

## Conscious Observation

To practice conscious observation, pick any object that you have lying around. It can be something that you use every day without even thinking about it, like your car keys, a pencil or your wallet. Now place the object in your hand and let it fully occupy your attention. Simply observe it for what it is, without labeling it or judging it in any way. Doing this will ground you in the present moment as you expand your attention to something outside of yourself. Conscious observation is a simple yet powerful form of meditation that will enable you to see deeper into the objects you are looking at.

## Sensory Mindfulness

Sensory mindfulness involves being mindful of the information that enters your brain through your five senses. Sensory mindfulness helps you develop an attunement to our own feelings, which results in deeper self-awareness and self-understanding. To practice sensory mindfulness, you can use specific stimuli to tap into each one of your senses:

- *Sight*: Take a walk in a garden and pay close attention to all the different shades of green that nature exhibits.

- *Scent*: Apply a lotion with a scent that you enjoy and be aware of the subtleties in smell as you rub it on your body.

- **_Hearing_**: Listen to an instrumental track and rest your awareness on the nuances in pitch, tone and beat of the music.

- **_Touch_**: Slowly stretch your limbs and pay attention to the sensations in them as you release tension in your body.

- **_Taste_**: Pick a fruit and resolve to eat it mindfully, savoring each nuance in flavor.

# Chapter 8 - Turning Mindfulness into a Habit

*"There are only two ways to live your life. One is as though nothing is a miracle. The other is as though everything is a miracle."*
Albert Einstein

The skill of mindfulness takes consistent practice and dedication to develop. It is not something you do one day and then forget about the next. In order to attain profound levels of presence, awareness, and inner peace you must practice mindfulness consistently.

In 2010, a study conducted at University College London showed that it takes on average 66 days to form a new habit. This means you need to invest about two months of effort before the behavior of mindfulness becomes automatic – something that you do without even thinking about it – a habit.

The key to making mindfulness automatic is to make it your top priority for the next 66 days. Mindfulness essentially has to become the most important activity in your day. Here are 7 ways to turn meditation into a habit:

## Work on Your "Why"

It is important that you get crystal clear on why you want to make mindfulness a habit. Are you driven to build more meaningful relationships, relieve stress, understand yourself better or be more productive? Whatever the reason is, make sure you have a deep burning desire to achieve your outcome. Once you have figured out your "Why", start visualizing your success. Imagine what your life would look like if you achieved your goal and use this mental image as fuel and motivation to keep you going throughout your mindfulness journey.

## Commit to the activity

Take a few seconds right now and make an oath to yourself that you are going to start incorporating mindfulness into your life every day from now on. Firmly resolve to follow though on this new habit and never give up. Feel the energy rising inside your body and seal the commitment with your heart.

## Start Small

There is no "right" amount of time to practice mindfulness for. If you're a beginner, don't fall into the trap of trying to be mindful absolutely all the time. Your mind simply isn't trained to sustain it. You can start with as little as 5 minutes using one of the mindfulness techniques mentioned previously. The key is not to overwhelm yourself when you're starting out.

## Decide on a fixed time and trigger

When developing a new habit, it's important to have a cue that reminds you to perform the new behavior around the same time everyday. As most of us already have well-established morning and evening routines, these are usually the easiest times to incorporate the practice of mindfulness. The key is to choose a trigger that makes it easy to juxtapose the new behavior onto an already existing habit. You could for example decide to practice mindful breathing right after you shower in the morning or you could mindfully brush your teeth everyday before you go to bed.

## Track Your Progress

Use a calendar to track your progress and make it visible. Mark down every single day that you follow through on your new habit. You'll be surprised how doing this will motivate you to keep going when the going gets tough as you will find it much harder to break your current streak. You can also use habit- tracking apps, which I have found to be extremely useful.

## Be Accountable

Find an accountability partner, preferably someone who is also looking to develop a long-term mindfulness practice. This will dramatically increase your chances of success. Humans by nature respond to social pressure so when you have someone that holds you accountable, you will find it a lot more difficult not to follow through.

## Reward Yourself

Whatever gets rewarded gets repeated. Your brain is constantly associating pain and pleasure to everything you do. So if you want your mindfulness habit to stick, trick your brain by rewarding yourself after you practice mindfulness. It can be as simple as congratulating yourself for being consistent or recompensing yourself with a treat.

Remember, consistent action is the only way to make mindfulness a habit. By practicing it everyday, you are effectively going create new neural pathways in your brain that will make the behavior automatic and you soon enough you won't even have to expand any willpower to engage in mindfulness. Make mindfulness a long-term habit and it will transform every aspect of your life.

# Conclusion

I hope this book was able to help you understand the power of integrating mindfulness into your daily life. The next step is to apply what you have learned and develop a long-term mindfulness practice. It can be a challenging process but I assure you that it is well worth it - You will make the most of every moment and enjoy a happier, more successful and balanced life free from stress, anxiety, and depression.

I wish you success on your mindfulness journey and I hope you quickly start reaping the amazing benefits that mindfulness has to offer.
Finally, if you enjoyed this book, then I'd like to ask you a favor. Would you be kind enough to share your thoughts and post a review of this book on Amazon?

Your voice is important for this book to reach as many people as possible. The more reviews this book gets, the more people will be able to find it and enjoy the incredible benefits of mindfulness.

Thank you for getting this book and good luck in your mindfulness journey!

# Bonus: Free Guided Meditation Series (5 Audiobooks)

→ Go to www.projectlimitlesslife.com/bonus-2 to get your FREE Guided Meditation Series.

You will get immediate access to:

- Healing Audio Meditation
- Higher Power Audio Meditation
- Potential Audio Meditation
- Quiet the Mind Audio Meditation
- Serenity Audio Meditation

You will also join my private kindle club and be the first to know about my upcoming kindle books.

→ Also Available on Amazon

# Preview of The Meditation Beginner's Bible

# Chapter 1 - What is meditation?

*"The gift of learning to meditate is the greatest gift you can give yourself in this lifetime."*
Sogyal Rinpoche

The word meditation and the word medicine come from the same Latin root "medicus" which means to cure. In the same way medicine cures sickness that exists inside the physical body by restoring it to a healthy state, meditation cures sickness that exists within the mind by returning it to its natural state of peace, joy and happiness.

*But how does the mind become sick?* Well, in our modern

society most of us suffer from what we call compulsive thinking. We have this inner voice that is constantly thinking, ruminating the past, worrying about the future, and hence we never fully experience the present moment.

Take a few seconds right now and become aware of your breathing. Observe the changing sensations of your breath as you inhale and then exhale. Be aware of your lungs filling and emptying themselves. Become one with your breath and notice the subtle gap between your incoming and outcoming breath - let yourself completely dissolve into the activity of breathing.

If you did this little exercise, I bet you noticed your mind becoming a bit more still. When you rest your attention on your breath, you effectively step away from the chaotic impulses of the mind and you connect to your true Self – that eternal part of you that is beyond the ephemeral, ever-wavering physical realm.

Meditation is essentially a vehicle for accessing a higher level of consciousness that is beyond thought, where you are reconnected to your deepest self, your true nature of joy, peace and happiness. When you meditate, you effectively increase your level of self-awareness and you awaken to the things that are beyond thought - love, beauty, peace... This cannot be rationalized intellectually; however it can be experienced when you bring stillness into your mind.

Moreover, meditation does not require effort. As mentioned earlier, it is not about trying to empty your mind. Spiritual leader Deepak Chopra puts it beautifully: "*Meditation is not a way of making your mind quiet. It is a way of entering into the quiet that is already there - buried under the 50 000 thoughts the average person thinks everyday.*"

When you practice meditation, you gain control over your mind, you break the cycle of seeking stimulation from the external world and you learn to draw your state from within. Meditation is truly a transformative experience that can have profound effects not just on your mind, but on virtually every aspect of your life – your body, relationships, health and even your career.

# Chapter 2 - The Benefits of Meditation

*"Meditation more than anything in my life was the biggest ingredient of whatever success I've had."*
Ray Dalio

Over the past decade, a vast amount of scientific research has been carried out to investigate the benefits of meditation for the human mind and body. The National Institute of Health has spent over $100 million toward research on meditation, and nowadays it seems like new studies professing the benefits of meditation are emerging everyday.

As a result of the various scientific discoveries on the benefits of meditation, a growing number of hospitals and medical centers are now teaching meditation to patients in order to address various health ailments, relieve pain and fight stress. For example, one famous meditation program called *Mindfulness Based Stress Reduction*, which was created in 1979 by Dr Jon Kabat-Zinn has become so popular that it is now offered in over 200 medical centers around the world.

One remarkable example of the effectiveness of meditation for pain relief is shown in a study conducted by Dr Fadel Zeidan at the Wake Forest Medical Center in North Carolina. In the study, 15 people who had never practiced meditation attended four, 20-minute mindfulness meditation classes. The participants' brain activity was examined before and after the training using magnetic resonance imaging. During both scans, they were exposed to a pain-inducing heat device. The results were impressive: After the training, the participant's pain intensity was reduced by about 40% and their pain unpleasantness by around 57%: 80 minutes of meditation was more effective than pain relieving drugs like morphine, which normally reduces pain by about 25%.

Meditation has also become popular in the corporate world, with some leading companies like Google providing meditation classes to their employees to relieve stress, improve focus and boost productivity. The search giant even took it a step further by building a labyrinth to encourage the practice of walking meditation. Moreover, Google is not the only company that is embracing meditation. In fact, other big corporations like Apple, Nike, Yahoo, McKinsey & Co... have all brought meditation to their workplaces in an endeavor to keep employees happy and productive.

Even schools are now adopting meditation to make kids calmer and more focused. Youth meditation program are being installed everywhere in the US, England, Canada and India. In 2014, Educational Psychology Review examined 15 peer-reviewed studies on meditation in schools and concluded that the practice had a myriad of positive effects on students, such as lessened anxiety, increased focus and stronger friendships.

Over 3,000 scientific studies have now been conducted on the benefits of meditation and the truth is practicing meditation has so many benefits that I could not list them all in this book. So here are 53 noteworthy benefits of developing a regular meditation practice:

## Health Benefits:

- Lowers blood pressure more effectively than medication
- Relieves pain more effectively than morphine
- Slows the progression of HIV
- Helps prevent fibromyalgia and arthritis
- Reduces risk of Alzheimer's
- Reduces risk of heart disease and stroke
- Provides rest deeper than sleep
- Helps recover from addiction
- Improves cardiovascular function
- Relieves irritable bowel syndrome
- Increases energy levels
- Slows down the aging process
- Improves athletic performance
- Improves quality of sleep
- Improves fertility
- Decreases muscle tension
- Improves skin tone
- Increases air flow to the lungs
- Boosts the immune system
- Reduces inflammation

# Mental and Emotional Benefits:

- Improves attention, focus and ability to work under pressure
- Helps manage ADHD
- Improves intelligence and memory
- Improves critical thinking and decision-making
- Fosters creativity
- Slows down cognitive decline
- Builds composure and calm in all situations
- Increases brain connectivity
- Improves mental strength
- Improves sex life
- Cultivates willpower
- Boosts cognitive function
- Increases grey matter in the hippocampus and frontal areas of the brain
- Helps manage emotional eating
- Promotes good mood
- Improves working memory and executive functioning
- Helps beat depression
- Reduces stress and anxiety
- Improves emotional stability
- Fosters empathy and positive relationships
- Decreases feelings of nervousness
- Reduces social isolation
- Enhances feelings of happiness and vitality
- Improves communication with other people
- Develops a sense of calm and serenity

# Spiritual Benefits:

- Enhances self-awareness
- Fosters peace of mind, happiness and joy
- Increases self-acceptance
- Boosts self-compassion
- Increases self-esteem
- Develops intuition
- Builds wisdom
- Increases capacity for love

→ Also Available on Amazon

Printed in Germany
by Amazon Distribution
GmbH, Leipzig